THIS IS A CARLTON BOOK

First published in 2002.
This edition published in 2013 by
Carlton Books Limited
20 Mortimer Street
London W1T 3JW

10 9 8 7 6 5 4 3 2 1

Text, illustrations and design copyright © 2002
Carlton Books Limited
Illustrations by Lucy Truman.

A CIP catalogue record for this book is available
from the British Library.

ISBN 978-1-78097-429-3

Printed and bound in China

Girl Drinks

101 cocktails for every occasion

rachel federman

CARLTON
BOOKS

contents

new york city

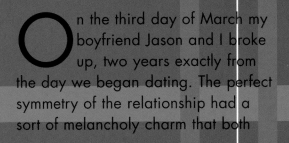

On the third day of March my boyfriend Jason and I broke up, two years exactly from the day we began dating. The perfect symmetry of the relationship had a sort of melancholy charm that both

cocktails

unnerved and satisfied me. After a week of sleepless, fevered nights, I ventured forth to begin getting over the break-up and researching this book, a fortunate coincidence of timing.

I went to bars all over New York in search of the perfect "girl drinks". My penchant for fancy mixed drinks had brought me years of criticism before they came into vogue, turning bartenders into celebrities overnight. Despite the wild surge in popularity of fancy drinks, some bartenders gave me blank looks when I asked about speciality cocktails, while others rattled off what was on tap that night. After a few false starts, I found exactly what I was looking for.

However, even in bars that offered an array of elaborate, brightly coloured mixed drinks, some visitors couldn't support the concept of girly cocktails. At Town at the Chambers Hotel, I described the project to a guy drinking vodka on the rocks. His reply: "You like drinks where you disguise the taste? If you're gonna take life, you've got to take it head on. Everything else is denial."

At the first bar I went to I asked for the house special.

Blank look.

"Do you have any favourites? Any exciting new cocktails?"

Same blank look.

"Can you recommend something?"

No response.

"Can you get me a mixed drink?"

They came up with an apple martini. By chance, I found out later, I had stumbled upon one of the hottest drinks in the bar scene on both coasts of the USA.

½oz/1.5cl vodka
1oz/3cl sour apple liqueur
Dash of lime juice
Slice of green apple to garnish

Shake with ice and strain into
a chilled martini glass.
Garnish with a slice of
green apple.

apple martini

caramel martini
@ UNION BAR

2oz/6cl vanilla vodka
1oz/3cl caramel syrup
Spun sugar to garnish

Shake and strain into a chilled martini glass and garnish with spun sugar.

Mandarin Martini

1½oz/4.5cl mandarin vodka
1oz/3cl peach schnapps
Dash of peach nectar
Dash of cranberry juice
Orange wedge to garnish

Shake vigorously and pour into a chilled martini glass, then add a fresh orange wedge.

Mother's Day
Martini

INVENTED BY ALBERT TRUMMER @ TOWN

3oz/9cl vodka
Dash of dry vermouth
Dash of rose water
3 fresh rose petals to garnish

Combine the ingredients in a mixing glass and gently stir.
Strain into a chilled martini glass and garnish with rose petals.

social climber

This may not take you higher up the social ladder,

but it will take you higher.

2oz/6cl raspberry vodka
½oz/1.5cl crème de cassis
½oz/1.5cl fresh lime juice
A few fresh raspberries

Shake the ingredients together with the raspberries,
and strain into a chilled martini glass.

Sex and the City Martini

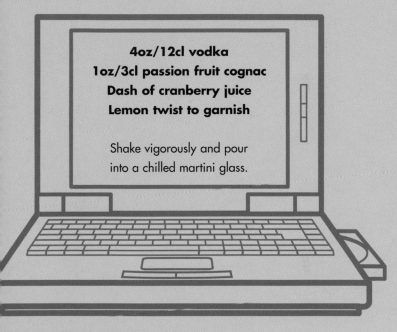

4oz/12cl vodka
1oz/3cl passion fruit cognac
Dash of cranberry juice
Lemon twist to garnish

Shake vigorously and pour
into a chilled martini glass.

*Joe Alberti created this drink after an episode of Sex and the City
was filmed in The Bar at the Stanhope. It takes nerve to name a
drink after the offbeat, award-winning show, but this new twist
on an old favourite lives up to its name.*

JADE BLISS

INVENTED BY JERRI BANKS @ CINNABAR

For this drink, you first need to make kaffir/lime mix.
To make enough for a large group you need:

Handful of kaffir lime leaves
8oz/24cl fresh lime juice
8oz/24cl simple syrup (equal parts granulated sugar
dissolved in hot water and left to cool)
4oz/12cl lime concentrate

Using a blender or food processor, blend the leaves, lime juice
and syrup, then strain and add the concentrate.

2oz/6cl citron vodka
1oz/3cl kaffir/lime mix
1oz/3cl green tea
Kaffir lime leaf (cut into thin ribbons) to garnish

Shake the ingredients vigorously with ice, then strain into a
chilled cocktail glass and garnish with ribbons of kaffir leaf.

Mojito

Mojitos are amazing, in the "this-is-so-good-I-had-no-idea-I-was-getting-this-drunk" variety, so be careful ...

2oz/6cl Bacardi limon
1oz/3cl dark rum
Freshly ground mint leaves
Fresh lime juice
Dash of lemon and lime soda
Teaspoon of sugar
Wedge of lime to garnish

Wet the rim of a chilled martini glass and dip it in sugar. Mix the ingredients together, strain into the glass and drop in a wedge of lime.

1oz/3cl Malibu rum
1oz/3cl vanilla vodka
1oz/3cl triple sec
Dash of orange juice
Cherry to garnish

cake

Shake the liquor and pour into a chilled martini glass, fill with orange juice and garnish with a cherry.

the columbian

INVENTED BY JENNIFER JOSEPH @ THE DINING ROOM

This is a delicious drink – and really cool to watch the espresso settle underneath the foam. Impress your friends!

1oz/3cl vanilla vodka
2oz/6cl white crème de cacao
1 shot of espresso

Mix the vodka and crème de cacao with ice in a shaker. Add the espresso and shake really vigorously until foamy. Wet the rim of a chilled martini glass and dip it in sugar, then strain the drink into it.

Chocolate-Covered Strawberry

INVENTED BY HEATHER CULTON
@ MADAME X

4oz/12cl vodka
2oz/6cl strawberry liqueur
1oz/3cl Godiva liqueur

Prepare on ice and strain into a martini glass.

Lava Gina

1oz/3cl Bacardi limon
3oz/9cl pissap
½oz/1.5cl lime juice
Dash of ginger extract
Orange twist to garnish

Mix the ingredients together and serve in an
oversized martini glass with an orange twist.

Town Passion

INVENTED BY ALBERT TRUMMER @ TOWN

Juice and seeds from 4 passion fruit
1oz/3cl lime juice
2 teaspoons simple syrup
(equal parts granulated
sugar dissolved in hot
water and left to cool)
¼oz/0.75cl tequila
¼oz/0.75cl cointreau
2oz/6cl champagne

Mix the passion-fruit juice and seeds, lime juice, simple syrup, tequila and cointreau in a food processor or blender. Strain, pour into a champagne glass filled with ice and add champagne.

the rossini

INVENTED BY ALBERT TRUMMER @ TOWN

1½oz/4.5cl fresh strawberry purée
1oz/3cl champagne

Mix in a shaker and strain into a champagne flute.

London Fog

For the original version of this classic, leave out the ice cream and simply shake the liquors with ice.

1oz/3cl white crème de menthe
1oz/3cl anisette
Dash of angostura bitters
1 scoop of vanilla ice cream

Blend until smooth and serve in a chilled cocktail glass.

shirley temple
black

According to the menu, this is a grown-up version of a classic cocktail.

@ THE DINING ROOM

2oz/6cl vanilla vodka
5 vodka-marinated sour cherries
Dash of club soda
Maraschino cherry to garnish

Marinate the sour cherries in vanilla vodka overnight. The next day, spoon them into a highball glass filled with ice, then pour in the vodka. Fill the glass with club soda and top with a maraschino cherry.

After my break-up with Jason, my band and I played a run of shows on the downtown circuit that were, by all accounts, our best performances to date. At first I couldn't imagine how I could get up on stage when I still felt so sad and out of focus, but the raw honesty of it all was exhilarating, as I guess I should have known it would be. All the broken-heart, ruined-love songs were entirely accurate. The period was further intensified by the *fin de siècle* feeling we had knowing that Joe, our lead guitarist and good friend, was going to leave the band.

For about a month or so, my lifestyle seemed to live up to the romantic ideal I'd had as a kid about living in New York after college. I was propelled along by the adrenaline rush after our gigs, free drinks everywhere I turned, and even the pathetic dissolution of my relationship, as all around me spring fever seemed to be in full swing.

1oz/3cl brandy
1oz/3cl black raspberry liqueur
1oz/3cl light rum

Between the Sheets in Rome

Mix together, pour over ice into a martini glass and drink in bed.

1½oz/4.5cl kahlua
1½oz/4.5cl orange liqueur
Slice of orange to garnish

Sex

Mix over ice and serve in a highball glass with a slice of orange.

SLOE COMFORTABLE SCREW

1oz/3cl vodka
⅔oz/2cl Southern Comfort
⅔oz/2cl sloe gin
Dash of fresh orange juice
Dash of grenadine

Pour the alcohol over ice into a highball glass, fill with orange juice and add a dash of grenadine.

get laid

1¾oz/5cl vodka
1oz/3cl raspberry schnapps
1oz/3cl pineapple juice
Dash of cranberry juice

Pour the ingredients over ice into a highball and stir.
Sip and make your move!

1oz/3cl kahlua
1oz/3cl orange liqueur
Dash of vanilla vodka
3oz/9cl milk

Gently heat the milk, kahlua and orange liqueur, and pour into a mug before it boils. Add a dash of vodka and serve by the fireplace.

sex in the
winter

sex on the beach

Mix in a glass with ice, top with soda water and serve with a pineapple wedge.

1oz/3cl vodka
½oz/1.5cl peach schnapps
½oz/1.5cl raspberry liqueur
5oz/15cl orange juice
Dash of soda water
Pineapple wedge to garnish

orgasm

1oz/3cl vodka
1oz/3cl kahlua
1oz/3cl amaretto
½oz/1.5cl orange liqueur
Dash of milk

Pour the liquor into a highball glass with ice and fill with milk.

climax

This has an alluring name, but given the combination of alcohol, you may finding yourself passing out before you can live up to it.

½oz/1.5cl vodka
½oz/1.5cl triple sec
½oz/1.5cl amaretto
½oz/1.5cl white crème de cacao
½oz/1.5cl banana liqueur
1oz/3cl milk

Shake with ice and strain into a chilled cocktail glass.

1oz/3cl midori
1oz/3cl blue curacao
1oz/3cl Malibu rum
1oz/3cl sloe gin
2½oz/7.5cl cranberry juice
½oz/1.5cl sour mix

lick

Shake the ingredients vigorously with ice
in a cocktail shaker and serve as shots.

INVENTED BY DARREN SUBARTON

¾ of a shot of espresso
1½oz/4.5cl vanilla vodka
¼oz/0.75cl kahlua
¼oz/0.75cl Tia Maria
¼oz/0.75cl Irish cream
3 espresso beans to garnish

Shake with ice. Strain and serve in a chilled martini
glass with three espresso beans.

the horny latte

INVENTED BY PHILIP CASACELI @ DADDY O

2oz/6cl pear liqueur
1oz/3cl light rum
½oz/1.5cl apple brandy
½oz/1.5cl banana liqueur
Dash of club soda

Pour all of the ingredients, except the soda, into a shaker with crushed ice. Shake, then strain and serve in a highball glass, topped with soda and a twisty straw.

SEXUAL TRANCE

1oz/3cl vodka
½oz/1.5cl melon liqueur
½oz/1.5cl raspberry liqueur
½oz/1.5cl orange juice
½oz/1.5cl pineapple juice
½oz/1.5cl lemon juice
Cherry or slice of orange to garnish

Shake with ice. Strain into an old-fashioned glass with ice and garnish with a cherry or orange slice.

wedding drinks

In June my roommate Kristin announced that she was getting married, and the rest of my friends started dropping like flies. In many cases, the engagement-news phone calls were the first time I'd heard from these people in several months. It wasn't my finest hour as a friend. The conversations all followed the same general pattern: "Hey – Rachel. You won't believe this, I'm getting married!" (Screams, laughter.) "What?" "Yeah! Mark

[Tim, Rob, Al, Mike, Matt] asked me last night! It's so crazy!" "Wow." "Can you believe it?" "Well, yeah. I guess. It's not that surprising." "I'm so happy! So how are things with Jason?" "We broke up." Awkward silence. "Really? Are you OK? I heard things are going really well with the band at least." "Joe's leaving." "No way! What are you going to do?" "Find another guitarist, I guess." "But how? That's impossible. You'll never find someone as good as Joe." Click.

The band had survived other behind-the-scenes dramas and I was sure we'd find a new guitarist, but the prospect of searching for one wasn't appealing, especially since things had been really looking up until Joe left. So, with my relationship splintered, everyone within a 20-mile radius registering their wedding lists at Crate & Barrel and the band teetering on the brink, I plunged into my mixed-drink research with renewed vigour. My focus turned to raspberry vodka, highball glasses, crème de cacao, Green Martinis, Sonic Blasters, Orange Bullets and the like.

adam  eve

1oz/3cl orange juice
1oz/3cl gin
½oz/1.5cl apricot brandy
½oz/1.5cl orange liqueur
Dash of lemon juice
Slice of apple to garnish

Shake with ice and strain into a cocktail glass.
Garnish with a slice of apple.

True Love

1½oz/4.5cl peppermint schnapps
1½oz/4.5cl white crème de cacao
Dash of soda water
Heart-shaped chocolate to garnish

Pour over ice in a highball glass, fill with soda water,
and garnish with a heart-shaped chocolate.

First Kiss

@ MADAME X

*A first kiss you can enjoy
more than once.*

**3oz/9cl dry white wine
Drop of rose syrup**

Serve in a wine glass with a cocktail stirrer.

kiss
in the
dark

1oz/3cl gin
1oz/3cl cherry brandy
1oz/3cl dry vermouth
2 maraschino cherries to garnish

Shake with ice. Strain into a cocktail
glass. Garnish with two maraschino
cherries. Serve by candlelight.

Mocha Kiss

1oz/3cl kahlua
1oz/3cl orange liqueur
2oz/6cl Irish cream
½oz/1.5cl mocha syrup
Dash of whipped cream and
shaved dark chocolate to garnish

Mix with ice and pour into an old-fashioned glass.
Garnish with whipped cream and shaved dark chocolate.

Crystal Slipper

1½oz/4.5cl gin
½oz/1.5cl blue curacao
2 dashes of orange bitters

Stir ingredients in a mixing glass with
ice, strain into a cocktail glass and toast
the happy couple.

Fantasy

4oz/12cl milk
1oz/3cl crème de menthe
½oz/1.5cl Irish cream
Chocolate sprinkles to garnish

Pour the milk into a mug and stir in the crème de menthe
and Irish cream. Serve with chocolate sprinkles.

I was shocked – shocked – to find out how quickly these go to your head!

2oz/6cl rum
1½ teaspoon grenadine
1½ teaspoon cherry liqueur
1½oz/4.5cl lime juice
Cherry to garnish

Shake with ice, garnish with a cherry and serve while listening to "As Time Goes By".

casablanca

l♥ve potion

1oz/3cl lime juice
2oz/6cl peach schnapps
2oz/6cl orange juice
2oz/6cl cranberry juice
3oz/9cl vodka
Cherry and slice
** of orange**
** to garnish**

Over the back of a spoon or a cherry, pour each layer into a glass in sequence. Serve with a glass of ice on the side garnished with a cherry, orange slice and cocktail umbrella. Pour the layered concoction over the ice and enjoy the magical effects.

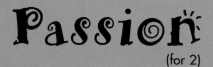

Passion

(for 2)

6oz/18cl passion fruit juice
4oz/12cl dark rum
Dash of cranberry juice
Dash of lemon juice
Dash of club soda
Cherry to garnish

Pour the passion fruit juice and rum over ice into a small bowl. Add the cranberry and lemon juices and top up with club soda. Serve garnished with a cherry and two long straws.

honeymoon

½oz/1.5cl Benedictine
½oz/1.5cl apple brandy
1 teaspoon triple sec
1 teaspoon fresh lemon juice

Shake with ice and strain into a cocktail glass.
Serve with a tropical umbrella garnish.

Remember: when reciting drinking records – achievements which
shouldn't be considered a testament to one's character and overall
success in life, but are often counted as such – make sure it is done
only at a bar where portions are well-regulated. Superhuman drinking
powers at weddings have been shown to be deceptive time and again
due to the plethora of watered-down drinks.

S ummer is arguably the best time for cocktails, with all the mouth-watering fresh fruit available and the long evenings creating an illusory sense of having more free time.

summer

vacation

drinks

Though it's been around for years and doesn't really have the chic-factor of the wild creations being served up in today's hotspots, the Midori Sour is probably my favourite summer drink. Unfortunately, it's now been added to the list of things that have taken on painful symbolic resonance after the break-up with Jason. When I met him, Jason was a staunch non-drinker. At his aunt's wedding during our first summer together, he took a few sips of my Midori Sour, then proceeded to drink the entire glass, so ending a 23-year-long bout on the wagon.

By the middle of the summer things were really starting to look up with the band. We'd found a great new guitarist, Alex, much faster than we'd anticipated. I was really excited about playing again – couldn't wait for rehearsals, couldn't calm down after they were over. One day walking to the subway I had the weirdest sensation – after those cold, dark months thinking I'd never like anyone again, it was starting to seem like maybe I did.

midori**sour**

2oz/6cl midori sour mix
Lemon and lime soda
Cherry to garnish

Pour the midori sour mix into a highball glass with ice
and fill with soda. Garnish with a cherry.

Long Island Iced Tea

My first real introduction to drinking came about 10 days into my first
year at college, in the form of a few watered-down beers followed by four
Long Island Iced Teas. I haven't been-over-the-top, off-the-wall drunk
more than three times in my life – but I started off with a bang. The first
time, I was only partly responsible: Long Island Iced Tea, I was told, was
just iced tea with a splash of vodka. Here's what it really is – and if you
don't think it contains enough liquor, some recipes add triple sec.

⅓oz/1cl vodka
⅓oz/1cl gin
⅓oz/1cl light rum
⅓oz/1cl tequila
Juice of half a lemon
Dash of cola
Slice of lemon to garnish

Pour all the ingredients into a
highball glass filled with ice.
Stir. Add a dash of cola and
a slice of lemon.

In Key West, the sunset is so spectacular that a huge crowd gathers every night on the pier to watch it. I've spent only one night there, and missed it by seconds. We heard the crowd clapping as we got out of the car and ran to the pier, but by that time the last rays of the sun had sunk below the horizon.

key west

1oz/3cl black raspberry liqueur
1oz/3cl light rum
2oz/6cl orange juice
1oz/3cl sour mix
5oz/15cl club soda
Slices of lime and orange to garnish

Mix in a tall glass with ice, then add lime and orange slices to garnish, and – if you have time – watermelon and cantaloupe balls.

St Croix Cocktail

INVENTED BY MICHAEL WATERHOUSE @ DYLAN PRIME

2oz/6cl banana rum
2oz/6cl fresh strawberry purée
½oz/1.5cl pineapple juice

Shake the ingredients in a cocktail shaker and strain over ice into a martini glass.

Bikini

2oz/6cl vodka
1oz/3cl light rum
½oz/1.5cl milk
1oz/3cl sour mix
1 teaspoon fine sugar
Juice of half a lemon
Slices of orange, lemon and lime to garnish

Shake with ice and pour into a cocktail glass. Garnish with lemon, orange and lime slices.

CREAMSICLE

For a true height-of-summer variation, try freezing the drink mixture in an ice-cube tray.

1oz/3cl light rum
½oz/1.5cl triple sec
½oz/1.5cl vanilla liqueur
Dash of orange juice
Dash of cream

Mix in a glass filled with ice, add equal parts of orange juice and cream. Shake until frothy and pour into a cocktail glass.

Coconut Crème Frappé

2oz/6cl rum
1oz/3cl Irish cream
1oz/3cl coconut cream
5oz/15cl milk

Shake all the ingredients with ice. Pour into a highball glass and serve with a straw and a cocktail umbrella.

BLUE HAWAII

½oz/1.5cl dark rum
½oz/1.5cl light rum
1oz/3cl blue curacao
1oz/3cl orange juice
1oz/3cl pineapple juice
Slice of orange and a cherry to garnish

Shake with ice and strain into a highball glass filled with ice. Serve with a slice of orange and a red cherry, or a slice of pineapple and coconut slivers.

In a metal shaker, crush the watermelon and mix with the sugar syrup. Add the ice and vodka. Shake vigorously and strain into a chilled martini glass. Garnish with a slice of watermelon.

watermelon martini

3 watermelon pieces
1oz/3cl sugar syrup
3oz/9cl vodka
Slice of watermelon to garnish

global blossom

INVENTED BY JERRI BANKS @ CINNABAR

To make the Sudanese hibiscus tea needed for this cocktail, place two tablespoons of hibiscus petals in a teapot and steep with 16oz/48cl of water for 10 minutes, then strain. Store it in the fridge and it will keep for 2–3 days.

1oz/3cl gin
2oz/6cl crème de cassis
1oz/3cl sudanese hibiscus tea
½oz/1.5cl lime juice
Dash of prosecco
Fresh edible flower to garnish

Pour the first four ingredients into a shaker, add ice and shake vigorously. Strain into a large saucer-type champagne or margarita glass filled with crushed ice. Top with prosecco and garnish with a fresh edible flower.

mint julep

The official drink of the Kentucky Derby. Over 80,000 are consumed over the two-day period of the Kentucky Oaks and Kentucky Derby.

Mint sprigs
1 teaspoon caster (superfine) sugar
1 tablespoon cold water
1¾oz/5cl bourbon

Place the fresh mint sprigs in a bowl with sugar and water. Crush the leaves with a spoon and stir. Pour bourbon over ice in a highball glass and add the mixture. Garnish with a fresh mint sprig and start the betting.

blueberry mojito
@ V-BAR

1½oz/4.5cl Bacardi rum
10 fresh blueberries
1oz/3cl sugar syrup
4 small pieces of lime
5 mint leaves (without stems)
Lemon and lime soda
Sections of lime to garnish

Pour the rum over ice in a cocktail shaker with the blueberries and sugar syrup, and shake vigorously. Crush the lime and mint leaves in a highball glass, pour in the rum mixture and ice and top with soda. Garnish with mint leaves and lime sections.

frozen
strawberry margarita

You can make raspberry or mango versions, too.

1oz/3cl tequila
¾oz/2cl triple sec
1oz/3cl lime juice
1oz/3cl orange juice
10 strawberries
Slice of lime to garnish

Rub a wedge of lime around the rim of a margarita glass and dip it into a saucer of coarse salt. Blend the ingredients with crushed ice. Pour into the glass and garnish with a slice of lime.

raspberry lime rickey

1oz/3cl raspberry vodka
1oz/3cl lemon and lime soda
1oz/3cl lime juice
Slice of lime to garnish

Mix the vodka and soda in a highball glass, then add the fresh lime juice. Garnish with a slice of lime.

Waltzing Matilda

4oz/12cl dry white wine
1oz/3cl gin
¼oz/0.75cl white curacao
1½oz/5cl fruit punch
Dash of club soda
Dash of grenadine
Orange peel twist to garnish

Shake the first four ingredients with ice and strain into a chilled highball. Fill with soda, add a dash of grenadine and drop a twist of orange peel into the glass.

lemon drop

3oz/9cl citron vodka
1oz/3cl Galliano
1 teaspoon of fresh lemon juice

Prepare a cocktail glass by rubbing the rim with a wedge of lemon and dipping it into a bowl of fine sugar. Shake the ingredients with ice and strain into the glass.

PARTY DRINKS

For a few weeks the impropriety of dating someone in my band kept me from telling anyone that I had a crush on Alex, the new guitarist. I finally told my roommates one Saturday afternoon while we were getting ready for a party we were having that night.

It was a great party; we reached a critical mass of people well before midnight, and it didn't taper off until after five in the morning. We had a DJ and big, splashy mixed drinks. The only disappointment – Alex never showed up. The next morning, as we began the excruciating task of clearing up and picking confetti off the floor, my roommates gave me the sympathetic shrug and eyebrow raise, as if to say: "Well, I guess now you know."

A week later, however, on a Sunday night after a 14-hour day recording at his place in Jersey, I went with Alex to a party in the East Village, showed the guests how to make Spanish Dynamites and Chocolate Martinis, and felt the tension rising. I was nervous and uncertain around Alex for the first hour or so, but let's just say that by the end of the night my roommates were proven wrong.

peppermint penguin

½oz/1.5cl green crème de menthe
1oz/3cl chocolate mint liqueur
3 Oreo cookies
2oz/6cl cream

Blend with ice, then serve in an old-fashioned ice cream-parlor glass with a long spoon.

Omaha Enchantment

⅓oz/1cl melon liqueur
⅓oz/1cl banana liqueur
⅓oz/1cl Irish cream
⅓oz/1cl pineapple juice

Shake with ice and strain into a cocktail glass. Add a green swizzle stick and toast the Union Pacific Railroad.

Baileys' Frappé

Pretty much anything with Baileys Irish cream in it qualifies as a top "girl drink", in my book.

Pour Baileys Irish cream over crushed ice. Serve in an old-fashioned milkshake glass with a straw.

Grasshopper

1oz/3cl green crème de menthe
1oz/3cl white crème de cacao
1oz/3cl double cream
or 2 scoops of vanilla ice cream

Shake with ice and strain into a cocktail glass.

MOULIN ROUGE

For a decadent whirlwind evening,
wake up your senses with this
heady cocktail.

1½oz/4.5cl sloe gin
⅔oz/2cl sweet vermouth
3 dashes angostura bitters

Shake with ice and strain into
a chilled cocktail glass.

Chocolate Martini

2oz/6cl vodka
½oz/1.5cl white crème de cacao or chocolate liqueur
Chocolate shavings or chocolate-dipped cherry to garnish

Pour vodka and white crème de cacao or chocolate liqueur over ice
in a mixing glass. Stir and strain into a cocktail glass. Garnish with
chocolate shavings or a chocolate-covered cherry.

When I told my dad I was writing this cocktail book, he reminded me of a strange drawing I made in third grade. On a family tree I drew my sister dancing, my mother cooking dinner and, God knows why, my father with his head thrown back, a bottle of Jack Daniel's upended in his mouth. I have never seen my father drink so much as a shot of hard alcohol, let alone guzzle JD straight from a bottle; I don't know what gave me the idea. You can imagine my parents' surprise when they saw the family trees hanging outside the classroom door on parent–teacher night.

Here is a cocktail my dad would never touch in a million years – named after the beach where he used to go as a kid:

Coney Island Hit-Parade

1½oz/4.5cl Irish cream
½oz/1.5cl black raspberry liqueur
Dash of grenadine
4 fresh raspberries

Mix the Irish cream, raspberry liqueur and a dash of grenadine over ice in an old-fashioned glass and add the raspberries.

oatmeal cookie

Now that cocktails are very much in vogue, the only ones that can still make people squirm and threaten any extant testosterone seem to be drinks with butterscotch schnapps. I suppose it just sounds too much like candy, and if that's what you want you really shouldn't be in a bar. Try asking for butterscotch schnapps and milk – it won't disappoint.

¼oz/0.75cl Jagermeister
½oz/1.5cl cinnamon schnapps
½oz/1.5cl Irish cream
½oz/1.5cl butterscotch schnapps

Shake with ice and serve as a shot.

carrot cake

1oz/3cl Iirish cream
1oz/3cl kahlua
1oz/3cl butterscotch schnapps
¼oz/0.75cl cinnamon schnapps

Shake with ice and serve in a chilled cocktail glass.

1oz/3cl hazelnut liqueur
1oz/3cl white crème de cacao
½oz/1.5cl milk

Shake with ice and strain into an old-fashioned glass.
Serve with a scoop of rocky road (almond, marshmallow
and chocolate) ice cream.

Rocky Road

SPANISH DYNAMITE

1oz/3cl tequila
½oz/1.5cl licor 43
½oz/1.5cl orange liqueur
1 scoop of orange sorbet
Cinnamon stick

Shake with ice, strain into a cocktail glass and stir
with a cinnamon stick.

Aunt Betty's
Apple Cider

*This is a perfect winter-warmer and delicious served
with gingerbread cookies.*

4oz/12cl apple cider
1½oz/4.5cl cinnamon schnapps
Dash of whipped cream
Cinnamon stick

Heat the cider gently in a saucepan, without letting it boil, and pour
it into a mug. Add the schnapps, top with whipped cream and stir
with a cinnamon stick.

hot peach cobbler

4oz/12cl apple cider
1½oz/4.5cl peach schnapps
Dash of cinnamon and a cinnamon stick
Scoop of vanilla ice cream (optional)

Gently heat the cider and pour into a mug. Add the peach
schnapps and a dash of cinnamon, and stir with a cinnamon stick.
Add a scoop of vanilla ice cream if you are feeling adventurous.

Piff's *espresso* martini

1 freshly made espresso
2oz/6cl vanilla vodka
1oz/3cl kahlua
1oz/3cl Irish cream

Shake the espresso, vodka and kahlua vigorously with ice, then strain into a martini glass. According to my bartender friend, Piff, "You'll produce a nice, long-lasting foam that will reside at the top of the glass." Then, slowly pour Irish cream into the middle of the glass, so that it settles at the bottom.

Mocha Mint

An ideal after-dinner drink.

1oz/3cl kahlua
¾oz/2cl crème de menthe
½oz/1.5cl white crème de cacao or chocolate liqueur

Mix in a shaker with ice and strain into a cocktail glass.

Rockaway Beach

Cross the Marine Park Bridge from Brooklyn to the Rockaways to discover strong surf and beautiful beaches. It's hard to believe you're still in New York City. This is where Alex and I went at midnight on our fourth date.

1oz/3cl light rum
½oz/1.5cl dark rum
1oz/3cl orange juice
½oz/1.5cl pineapple juice
½oz/1.5cl cranberry juice
Dash of crème de noyaux
Cherry to garnish

Mix all of the ingredients in a cocktail shaker with ice and shake. Strain into a highball. Garnish with a cherry.

Batida de Coco

2oz/6cl Malibu rum
2oz/6cl passion fruit juice
Dash of condensed milk

Mix the rum and fruit juice with ice in a tumbler, and add condensed milk to taste. For a party, make the above recipe times eight and serve in a pitcher.

By late summer, our band Dimestore Scenario played uptown for the first time since we began, at Le Bar Bat on West 57th. The place was beautiful and massive (compared to the downtown places we were used to playing), with blue bats hanging from the ceiling, a balcony and an upstairs lounge.

Both our first drummer, Ivan, and original guitarist, Joe, were in the audience, as was the guitarist from Johnny Leisure, a band I'd played with in college, but the spectre of the past no longer seemed to matter. The distance between this gig and the ones when we knew Joe was leaving was vast. Things were great with Alex, the band had finally found the perfect line-up, the songs were tight, and Le Bar Bat asked us back for a Saturday night. I was too excited to sleep after that show; it felt like we were on the verge of something really big.

casino

2oz/6cl gin
⅓oz/1cl maraschino cherry liqueur
⅓oz/1cl lemon juice
2 dashes of orange bitters
Maraschino cherry to garnish

Shake with ice and strain into a cocktail glass.
Top with a maraschino cherry.

Black Jack

1oz/3cl blackberry brandy
½oz/1.5cl Jagermeister
1oz/3cl double cream

Shake with ice and strain into a chilled
cocktail glass with crushed ice.

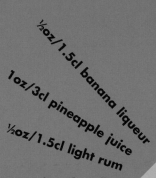

½oz/1.5cl banana liqueur
1oz/3cl pineapple juice
½oz/1.5cl light rum
½oz/1.5cl vodka

1oz/3cl orange juice
1oz/3cl cranberry juice
Slices of orange and
lime to garnish

Shake with ice and
strain into a highball
glass filled with ice.
Top with orange and
lime slices.

Sonic Blaster

Like its namesake, this drink is a high-flying bomber.

½oz/1.5cl amaretto
½oz/1.5cl kahlua
½oz/1.5cl Irish cream

B-52

Mix ingredients in a shot glass and serve.

bolero

1½oz/4.5cl light rum
⅔oz/2cl apple brandy
¼oz/0.75cl sweet vermouth

Pour all the ingredients into a mixing glass with crushed ice and stir well. Strain into an old-fashioned glass with ice cubes.

Lady Be Good

*Ice cream is a great complement to this combination
of alcohol, and you can never get too much of a good thing.*

1½oz/4.5cl brandy
½oz/1.5cl white crème de menthe
½oz/1.5cl sweet vermouth
1 scoop of mint chocolate ice cream

Shake the brandy, crème de menthe and vermouth with ice.
Strain into a cocktail glass and top with the ice cream.

Blue Velvet

2½oz/7.5cl vodka
½oz/1.5cl blue curacao
2oz/6cl lime juice
Slice of lime to garnish

Shake with ice in a cocktail shaker, strain into
a cocktail glass and garnish with a slice of lime.

Black Magic

1½oz/4.5cl vodka
½oz/1.5cl kahlua
Dash of lemon juice
Slice of lemon to garnish

Shake with crushed ice and strain into an old-fashioned glass.
Garnish with a slice of lemon.

"The White Spider" was recommended to me by my downstairs neighbour Greg Chow, the erotic drinks columnist for Mojo magazine – I'm not sure how it qualifies as erotic.

the white spider

2oz/6cl vodka
1oz/3cl white crème de menthe

Shake with ice, strain and serve in a martini glass.

pink squirrel

1oz/3cl white crème de cacao
1oz/3cl crème de noyaux
1oz/3cl double cream
⅓oz/1cl grenadine

Mix the ingredients with ice in a shaker or blender. Strain into a chilled cocktail glass.

le Passage

This unusual combination was suggested to a bartender friend of mine by a mysterious but quite affable woman in a see-through dress while he was tending bar at Le Passage, Chicago.

2oz/6cl Irish cream
2oz/6cl Malibu rum

Shake vigorously with ice and strain into a chilled martini glass.

Winter in Brazil

2oz/6cl Malibu rum
Mug of hot chocolate
Dash of whipped cream
Chocolate shavings to garnish

Pour the rum into the hot chocolate and top with whipped cream and shaved chocolate pieces.

olympia

1½oz/4.5cl midori
1oz/3cl Malibu rum
½oz/1.5cl light cream

Blend with crushed ice, pour into a highball glass
and serve with a green swizzle stick.

1oz/3cl orange liqueur
⅔oz/2cl kirsch
½oz/1.5cl green chartreuse
3 dashes of maraschino cherry liqueur

Shake with ice and strain into a chilled cocktail glass.

lollipop

Brighton Beach

This is a strong one. Drink more than one of these and you might fall asleep under the boardwalk.

⅔oz/2cl brandy
⅔oz/2cl benedictine
⅓oz/1cl bourbon
1oz/3cl sour mix
2oz/6cl orange juice
1oz/3cl soda water

Mix the brandy, benedictine and bourbon with ice. Add the sour mix, orange juice and soda water, then shake. Pour into a highball glass and top with a cocktail umbrella.

Virginia Rebel Yell

1oz/3cl whiskey
1oz/3cl Irish cream
1oz/3cl hazelnut liqueur
Dash of milk

Mix the ingredients with ice, strain into a cocktail glass and add milk to taste.

G iven the unreal pace of events, I shouldn't have been surprised when two weeks after the gig at Le Bar Bat our drummer, Than, left to devote more time to one of his many other bands. We still needed a band photo; the shoot was like going to a wedding with an ex just after you break up because it's easier than making other plans.

CLASSIC MIXED DRINKS

Afterwards, I went for a drink by myself in a bar overlooking the East River and thought about the time Jason had hidden flowers under the Brooklyn Bridge for me. In many ways, I suppose, the relationship was still mapped out over the epic proportions of this chaotic, beautiful city. After the weird, nostalgic feeling of the photo shoot, with Than's absence looming, I expected to feel really down, but I didn't at all. So many ends to so many eras, but for the first time in a while I felt strangely at peace with it.

A guy in a "Put Out Records" T-shirt approached me and asked what I was drinking. I'd had so many ornate and wildly creative drinks since I began writing this book, but the first time someone asked what I was drinking, it was just a Whiskey Sour, a simple, classic mixed drink. I told him and he ordered one from the bartender, then gave me the thumbs up. I figured I might as well ask him if he played the drums. It was a long shot, but you never know ...

screwdriver

5oz/15cl fresh orange juice
1½oz/4.5cl vodka
Slice of orange to garnish

Pour the juice and vodka over ice into a highball glass. Garnish with a slice of orange.

Whiskey Sour

1½oz/4.5cl whiskey
1½oz/4.5cl sour mix
Dash of lemon juice
Cherry and slice of orange to garnish

Shake with ice and strain into a cocktail glass. Garnish with a cherry and a slice of orange.

Tom Collins

2oz/6cl gin
2oz/6cl sour mix
Dash of soda water
Slice of orange and a cherry to garnish

Pour the gin over ice into a collins glass. Add the sour mix and a dash of soda. Garnish with a slice of orange and a cherry.

Cape Codder

1¼oz/3.75cl vodka
3oz/9cl cranberry juice
Dash of lime juice
Slice of lime to garnish

Pour the vodka over ice, add cranberry juice and a dash of lime juice. Garnish with a slice of lime.

Madras

A Madras is also known as a California Breeze. Use grapefruit juice instead of orange and it becomes a classic Sea Breeze.

2oz/6cl vodka
2oz/6cl orange juice
1oz/3cl cranberry juice
Slices of orange and lime to garnish

Pour the vodka and juices into a highball filled with ice. Garnish with a slice of orange and a slice of lime.

White Russian

As my neighbor Greg Chow wrote in his column for Mojo magazine:
"Everyone laughs at White Russians, but mostly everyone actually
enjoys them. People are just afraid to order them. So despite what
bartenders, girls and your friends will tell you, it takes a real man
to drink a White Russian."

1oz/3cl vodka
1oz/3cl kahlua
Dash of milk

Pour the vodka and kahlua into an old-fashioned glass with ice.
Then fill it up with milk.

toasted almond

1oz/3cl kahlua
1oz/3cl amaretto
Dash of milk

Mix the kahlua and amaretto with ice and
strain into a cocktail glass. Add milk to taste.

Frozen
Pina Colada

1¾oz/5cl light rum
1¾oz/5cl coconut cream
3oz/9cl pineapple juice
Slice of pineapple, a cherry and
  shredded coconut to garnish

Blend with crushed ice until smooth, then pour into a colada glass
and garnish with pineapple, a cherry and shredded coconut.

Kir

5oz/15cl dry white wine
½oz/1.5cl crème de cassis

Mix the chilled ingredients and
serve in a wine glass.

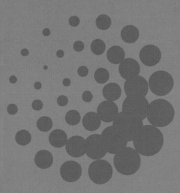

Kir Royal

2oz/6cl champagne
Dash of framboise

Pour the champagne into a flute and
add a dash of framboise for colour.

strawberry daiquiri

1¾oz/5cl light rum
1oz/3cl lemon juice
8 strawberries
1 teaspoon caster (superfine) sugar
Slice of lime and a strawberry to garnish

Blend the ingredients until smooth. If the mixture is too thick, add a
little water; if it's too thin, add some more ice. Pour into a cocktail
glass and garnish with lime and a strawberry, then add a straw.

Manhattan

The Manhattan Club created this drink to entertain politician, Samuel J Tilden.

1½oz/4.5cl whiskey
⅔oz/2cl sweet vermouth
Dash of angostura bitters
Cherry or lemon twist to garnish

Stir with ice and strain into a chilled cocktail glass.
Garnish with a cherry or lemon twist.

Irish coffee

Americans often lace this drink with green crème de menthe but, as a rule, the Irish look down on this practice. The traditional drink uses hot coffee, but it's also great with iced coffee.

2oz/6cl Irish whiskey
Hot coffee
2 teaspoons caster
 (superfine) sugar
Dash of double cream

Pour the whiskey, sugar and coffee into a mug, or a glass rinsed with boiling water, and stir. Pour the cream over the back of a teaspoon held just above the coffee mixture so that it floats on top. The trick is to sip the drink through the layer of cream.

Index

Acknowledgments

Cinnabar
235 West 56th Street,
New York, NY 10019
*Jade Bliss, p 12, and Global
Blossom, p 50
(both invented by Jerri Banks)*

Daddy O
44 Bedford Street,
New York, NY 10014
*The Horny Latte, p 28
(invented by Philip Casaceli)*

The Dining Room
154 East 79th Street,
New York, NY 10021
*The Columbian, p 15
(invented by Jennifer Joseph),
and Shirley Temple Black, p 19*

DYLAN Prime
62 Laight Street,
New York, NY 10013
*St Croix Cocktail, p 45
(invented by Michael
Waterhouse)*

Madame X
94 West Houston Street,
New York, NY 10012
*Chocolate-Covered Strawberry,
p 16 (invented by Heather
Culton), and First Kiss, p 34*

Pop
127 4th Avenue,
New York, NY 10003
Mojito, p 14

Town
The Chambers Hotel,
15 West 56th Street,
New York, NY 10019
*Mother's Day Martini, p10,
The Rossini, p17, and Town
Passion, p17 (all invented by
Albert Trummer)*

Union Bar
204 Park Avenue South,
between 17th and 18th Street,
New York, NY 10003
Caramel Martini, p 9

V-Bar
3355 Las Vegas Boulevard,
Las Vegas, NV 89109
Blueberry Mojito, p 51

Drinks
Climax, p 27, adapted from
The Bartender's Black Book,
5th Edition, Stephen Kittredge
Cunningham, The Black Book
Co., 2000

Waltzing Matilda, p 54, Mocha
Mint, p 67, Casino, p 72, and
Sonic Blaster, p 74, adapted
from **www.mixed-drink.com**

Thanks to:
Mixed-drink.com,
Mojo Magazine, Piff,
Greg Chow, The Bartender's
Black Book, Stephen Kittredge
Cunningham, The Black Book
Co., 2000.